"*Awaken to Your Dreams* takes you on a journey of self-discovery and provides you with the steps to be the best version of yourself. There are goosebump moments in Ron's book as you relive his journey from prison to his life today. Ron's book is inspirational and well worth the read."

—Kristen Tillona Baker
Executive Director, Mary Lyon Foundation

"Working as a financial advisor for almost 40 years, I have been to many industry conventions and seminars designed to improve my practice. But most of the time I come back home and, though I heard some great ideas, seldom incorporate them into my practice. Have you experienced this in your life? I believe this book by Ron L. James will help you to take action to change your life in a positive way. It will put you on the path to be the person that you want to be."

—David S. Kratz
Financial Consultant

"*Awaken to Your Dreams* is a compelling guide to unlocking your true potential and living a life of purpose. Ron L. James masterfully combines personal anecdotes, insightful reflections and practical exercises to empower readers to break free from the limitations of their past and step into the limitless possibilities of their future. Through the power of imagination, faith and positive affirmations, James inspires readers to envision their dreams and take bold steps towards achieving them. This book is a powerful tool for anyone ready to embark on a journey of self-discovery, transformation and fulfillment. Prepare to be inspired, motivated and empowered to awaken to your dreams!"

—Kasey King
Realtor, Iron Valley Real Estate

"Ron James's beautifully written and inspiring testimony demonstrates how we, ourselves, hold the power to change our lives. In being self-reflexive and transparent about his own personal 'choices,' good and bad, James provides us a real-life roadmap for how to develop transformative change within ourselves. This guidance for 'empowerment to change and grow' is both practical and doable. Choose to read this book!"

—Patrice Jeppson, PhD
Researcher, Anthropological

"I had the pleasure of reading Ron L. James's manuscript, *Awaken to Your Dreams*, in one sitting, and I must say it was an impactful and concise read! James's writing style, with its storytelling approach, not only made the reading enjoyable but also delivered a clear and inspirational message. His words and stories affirm the boundless potential within each of us, reminding us that, with determination, anything is possible. *Awaken to Your Dreams* is a must-read for anyone seeking inspiration and empowerment."

—Stephanie Werner
Realtor, Berkshire Hathaway

AWAKEN TO YOUR DREAMS

Looking Inside Yourself to Navigate Life's Path

RON L JAMES

Foreword by Don Schin

Paperback ISBN 978-1-960007-44-5
eBook ISBN 978-1-960007-45-2

In Partnership with
Ron L. James CHOICES
PO Box 7402
York, PA 17404

&

Orison Publishers, Inc.

PO Box 188
Grantham, PA 17027
www.OrisonPublishers.com

DEDICATION

I dedicate this book to the unsung hero in my life,
my not-much-talked-about dad, John Willis James,
affectionately known as Johnny. His entrepreneurial spirit
is etched in my DNA, and his ability to think outside
and inside the box has shaped who I am today.
He navigated life with wit and precision, always imparting
wisdom to those around him. His laughter inspired
and encouraged others to see the best in themselves.

Special thanks also go to Annie Wilcox
for her exceptional ability to wordsmith and assist
with editing, adding depth and clarity to this work.

CONTENTS

FOREWORD

I always advise people to work with someone who has "been there and done that"—someone who has walked in the shoes you want to walk in, owned the type of business you're thinking about opening, led the organization you're thinking about leading. I also think that there is no failure in life if you can look at the experience and learn from it. So, when seeking advice or counsel, look at what people have done themselves. That's what I think of when I think of Ron James. Good and bad, James has been there, done it, lived it and learned from it. What Ron writes about in all of his books, and particularly in *Awaken to your Dreams*, is real, it's useful and it's applicable to all of us. He shares his learning from it all as well as the tools he developed along the way. The tools are important; they have helped him pull himself up out of a dangerous, toxic, downward spiral and make himself into a highly successful man in all of his roles in life: husband, father, friend, businessman, life coach, speaker and author. I encourage you, if you are serious about changing your life, to read this book and use the tools inside it.

Don Schin
CEO, Franchise Building Expert

PROLOGUE

NAPOLEON HILL

Malcolm Gladwell states the "ten thousand rule" in his 2008 book, *Outliers: The Story of Success*. He cites studies done on violinist performers and composers who practiced for thousands of hours as youngsters to perfect their craft. The distinguished Gladwell writes that "ten thousand hours is the magic number for greatness."[1]

Since my release from prison on May 14, 2012, I have been on a personal quest to become the absolute best version of

---

1 Malcolm Gladwell, *Outliers: The Story of Success* (New York: Little, Brown and Company, 2008), 38-39.

myself by working daily toward those ten thousand hours of greatness. A vital part of my quest is putting to rest the old idea that I had to chase after what I envisioned other people thought I should do and instead doing what I wanted to do. What I want to do is help you become good at whatever it is *you* want in your life!

In the four decades prior to my release from prison, I chalked up many losses, failures and shortcomings. However, because of the severe consequences they brought, they also enabled me to discover my true purpose here on earth: helping you become your best self.

I believe wholeheartedly that anyone who reads this book can learn from its contents. There is a quotation that rings true regarding everything I have ever done to acquire wealth, peace, prosperity and success. That quote is, "Knowledge without implementation is a total waste of time."[2] Now, ninety-nine-point-nine percent of the people I personally know, and probably the same percentage of people you know, have similar or the same problems that they need to do something about. What that "something" is will vary from situation to situation, person to person, and problem to problem. However, the fact remains that most people will see a problem. Then they will read about that problem. They will research that problem. They will talk to anybody and everybody about that problem, and the religious folk will even pray about that problem. Yet, at the end of the day, nothing changes. The reason that nothing changes is that most people hate change. *Hate* is a very strong word, so I will elaborate.

Millions of people each year decide to go on a diet. Most of them, or a great majority of them, move in this direction come January 1st each year. America is full of New Year's resolutions that, for whatever reason, are broken within forty-eight hours

---

2 Bruce Lee has been attributed with saying, "Knowledge with application is useless," but the quote most likely goes farther back to Abu Bakr.

of their beginning. Ask yourself when the last time was that you took on a New Year's resolution—and how long did it take for you to break it?

We in the James family love a challenge, and every year we like to take on new, New Year's resolutions. However, you won't find us moving in the direction of a new diet. Why? The reason is we have redefined our mindset when it comes to the word *diet*. We have transformed our thinking and replaced the word *diet* in terms of optimal health. In other words, we eat not just to eat, or even because we're hungry; rather, we eat to fuel our bodies so that we can have the proper nutrition and balance for a healthy lifestyle. Usually, when people think of the word *diet*, it brings up a picture of a yo-yo going up and down, up and down. So, the word *diet* is not entertained in the James family. The change in our minds has created a healthy lifestyle so that no on-and-off yo-yo effect can take place.

Individuals look to change leading up to the week before starting their New Year's resolution. They want to change, but before they do, they eat like crazy during the holidays—overindulging in every area of life. If they are drinkers, they drink alcohol; if they like sweets, they eat candy and cookies; if they're eating out, they double dip on double portions and take one more trip to the dessert table. It is almost as if people will eat until they are sick and then justify their good meal! This process may occur four or five times with friends and family, at company parties, at the in-laws or just because.

Their intentions are better than good; in fact, they're great! People's spirits are flying high, and so are the New Year's celebrations. The ball drops, the horns blow, the excitement grows, and then it is time to face the music. The clock turns to 12:01 a.m. and New Year's resolutions are supposed to go into effect. However, some people might not start just yet because they hung out too late. Some grab their heads with hangovers. Others sleep in because of parties, and, for whatever reason, any old excuse will do to put off that resolution one more day. But, be assured, when they do get started, they are all in! The new gym membership is paid for. The new bike is ready to go. The latest treadmill is set up. A new weight belt and gloves for the gym are waiting. At last, people finally act. Yet, the action they finally take is not deep-rooted. Instead, the rut that is deep-rooted is the one that takes over. Somehow, some way, most people quit, give up and find an excuse to justify it.

These actions—what you do before and right after New Year's—are what I call "surface" actions or "feel-good" actions. These are the actions that have only a momentary, or slight, effect. About day three of your life-changing diet, workout or whatever you promised yourself you were going to do, you acquire a new thought. I call it the "peekaboo" thought. It is an idea people succumb to all too easily. "I deserve a break. I have been working hard. One little this or one little that won't hurt. One more won't matter. I will start tomorrow."

These subtle peekaboo thoughts notoriously show up disguised as non-threatening, cute, adorable puppies. All the time, these thoughts are actually as powerful as raging wolves that cannot wait to devour you and hold you at bay until your demise. Your reality will always be the way you understand life. Reality is different for every individual, and, in the case of a diet, your reality will always be how you see it. The fact is, nothing changes if nothing changes. This sounds like a simple statement that is easy to understand, but as a powerful adage it deserves focused attention.

In the following chapters, I will share with you a surefire way to change your mindset and set a new course of direction that will cause you to take new action. And as a self-proclaimed motivational speaker, inspirational speaker and authentic storyteller, it would be a travesty for me to not share the finer details of my horrific, life-shattering and, at times, life-threatening past. We will delve into my past one layer at a time to thoroughly understand what caused the extreme chaos that led to a clouded and confused imagination that, if not addressed, arrested and *changed*, would have brought me to my own demise—an early grave.

New actions result in new effects that bring change to your life. It is time to breathe life into your dreams.

Chapter One

ACTIONS FOLLOW BELIEFS

"ATTENTION IS THE KEY TO LIFE. WHATEVER YOU
REALLY GIVE YOUR ATTENTION TO,
YOU BECOME. WHATEVER YOU REALLY
CONCENTRATE UPON WILL COME INTO YOUR LIFE.
WE GROW INTO THE THING THAT FILLS OUR
THOUGHTS AS INEVITABLY AS THE STREAM
MERGES INTO THE OCEAN AT LAST."

———————

EMMET FOX

In my book, *A Year of Choice, A Year of Change: Success Made Easy Through Monthly, Weekly, and Daily Practices*, I talk about a process I coined as "See It, Say It, Speak It, Be It." This process, if implemented, can aid in an individual's becoming extremely successful and/or changing one's self and mindset. Following is how it works.

See It! I know what is needed to create change in my life. *Doing* what is needed is another story. However, at some point, one or two things occur. First, I get sick and tired of being sick and tired, and second, I say, in effect, "Enough is enough." I *decide* to make a change. I also could be overwhelmed by life circumstances, which motivates me to make a massive change. In either case, a desire occurred that motivated me. I now *see it*. I see the desire, and the pendulum starts to swing and move in a new direction.

Say It! Now, as I begin to speak life into every situation, I begin to see things as I encourage myself. This is where I *say it*. It comes off in a tone that rings out like this: "I can do it!" "I will do it!" "I am not quitting!" That conversation is one of self-confidence and encouragement. The pendulum keeps moving in the other direction from where I was, gaining momentum toward my desired goal.

Speak It! If you look at the four stages of competence—unconscious competence, conscious competence, unconscious incompetence and conscious incompetence—you realize that "*speak it*" is where conscious competence comes in. You begin to understand how and why you make the changes necessary to keeping the pendulum moving in a favorable direction.

Be It! This stage occurs when you know you have created a new mindset, a new change, a game-changing change! You know that no one can come up behind you, or even next to you, and tell you something that will unnerve you. *You will "say it" because you see it, and you see it because you have said it.*

I once heard a story of some young kids who wanted to play a practical joke on their parents and family members. The family had taken a vacation on a cruise ship and sailed off out to sea. A glorious vacation! About a day later the cruise headed into some slightly choppy waters. The ship was rocking and swaying a little more than usual. The youth had come up to the deck of the cruise ship where they agreed to play this prank on one of their family members, the father of one of the boys. In succession, each of the youth made comments to him. The son started out, "Dad, are you okay? You don't look so good." The father proceeded to question himself about what was said but chalked it up as not being such a big deal. However, a few moments later the nephew showed up and said, "Uncle Jim, are you okay? You don't look well. You look very pale, as a matter of fact. You must be sick." This joke was not complete until the niece came strolling by and sealed the deal with, "Uncle Jim, you look seasick!" Jim headed back to his cabin, wobbling to and fro as the ship swayed. He passed his wife on her way up to the deck with her hat, sunglasses, sunscreen and bag in tow. She said to Jim, "Let's go up on the deck." To her surprise, Jim answered, "No, I'm not feeling so good. I think I'm seasick!" This practical joke placed Jim in the cabin, in the bathroom and in front of the mirror. For a good portion of the cruise, Jim ran back and forth into his cabin to throw up.

The family members continued their antics and decided to play the same trick on Uncle Bob. However, Uncle Bob was an ex-Navy Seal and a retired mariner of the Merchant Marine. You can imagine when the same comments were directed toward Bob, the joke had quite a different outcome. Bob knew who he was. He had spent many years, months, days and nights sailing the seas. What was meant to be a practical joke for Bob was immediately dismissed as foolish nonsense. Uncle Bob went about his vacation as he had planned.

"*Be it*" is owning what you say. Both Jim and Bob owned, or heard, what their inner voice told them about which direction they were going to go. Jim's inner voice led him to the cabin toilet, while Bob's led him to a cool drink at the bar on the deck. In my book, *A Year of Choice, A Year of Change*, I expound about the two voices that speak to us. The first is the voice of "the Builder." The Builder is the voice that will ultimately lead you toward your life's dreams, aspirations, visions, goals and desires. That voice feeds our fate and moves us in the direction we claim we want to go. The second voice I label as "the Sniper." The Sniper is the voice we are all too familiar with. This voice attacks, hinders, destroys, disables and kills the inner self's dreams, aspirations, visions, goals and desires. The Sniper is the voice that feeds the ever-consuming nemesis known to all mankind as fear! In my pursuit to discover why I would willingly choose the voice of fear over the voice of faith (which was beyond me), and after intense mining and digging for the answer, I believe I have stumbled upon a relatively simple reason.

"Fat Ronnie"

First, I worked hard at choosing a life of fear. I became, as Malcolm Gladwell puts it, an expert. I don't mean that I was fearful of my own shadow—with or without the lights turned on—like the scaredy cat you see running away from what startled it. No, I lived completely the opposite. In fact, in some areas of my life, I was as fierce as a lion. However, when it came to my self-esteem, I had somehow adopted the belief that I was "less than." One example of this tragic self-shame occurred in my household. Growing up, I was known as "Fat Ronnie." The name was not a dig at my character; it was who I said I was at that time. This label became my identity and is my first memorable "I am" statement. This "I am" statement has taken me a lifetime to understand, analyze, rethink, process and rewire to redefine, redirect and regain a better version of myself. I desired and chose a better version of myself, and that is what I now imagine as my true "I am"!

The label "Fat Ronnie," as innocent as that name may seem, was horrifying and extremely damaging to my self-worth. It all came about because there just so happened to be four Rons in our family. The oldest Ron, or Ronald, was my uncle.

Everyone identified him as Uncle Pete. Some called him "Peter Rabbit." My uncle was extremely gifted and talented, and I admired him. I identified myself and lined myself up with his character. I actually am named after both my uncles. My father's brothers were Uncle Ronald (Uncle Pete) and Uncle Lloyd. Thus my birth name is Ronald Lloyd James. The next Ron in line in our family was my older cousin. He was older than me by several years and was born to my uncle's first wife. He was the first boy in that line after Uncle Pete. To identify him, because he was very fair skinned, everyone called him "Light-Skinned Ronnie." To add challenges to all the James family, a younger Ronald came on the scene through an additional relationship that Uncle Pete had formed with Aunt Roselyn, who had two sons, Gerald and Ronald. This Ronald was known as "Little Ronnie."

So we had Uncle Pete, who was the oldest Ronald. He had two sons, both named Ronald: Light-Skinned Ronnie and Little Ronnie. Then there was me. Because I was heavier, everyone called me "Fat Ronnie." I was called Fat Ronnie to help differentiate me from the others with the same name in the family—nothing more; nothing less. However, I owned that label. I was overweight as a child and struggled with that identity for years. My conscious mind fed my subconscious mind with thoughts that I needed to be this big, fat guy to have a place within my family circle. I overate and gorged myself. My appetite increased, and I continued to eat more and more. I wore 2X- and 3X-sized clothing, told myself that I was big-boned, and, worst of all, that I was Fat Ronnie. I became who I said I was. Remember, I was putting in the work and the hours to prove it.

Second, even more terrifyingly, by the time I reached the fourth grade I believed a new lie. It all started in the summer after my second-grade year. My parents wanted a better life for me and my four siblings, so we moved from the City of Brotherly Love, known to everyone as Philadelphia. The move from the city seemed promising. We ended up in one of the most prestigious developments in Montgomery County, Pennsylvania. It was called Pennwood Gardens.

I noticed immediately that I was in water over my head. Upon admission for the start of the new school year, I was required to take some aptitude tests to see where I would best fit in. The tests didn't go well. As a result, I was required to essentially repeat the second grade, and I certainly was not happy about it. I did not understand why, since I had just finished the second grade, I now had to do it all over again. Not to mention, I also happened to be "the only." What is "the only"? Well, in my case, I was the only black male in my school. The only other black person in the school was my younger sister. On top of that, I wore the label, "fat." So there I was, fat, black and put back to repeat the second grade.

I am certain my parents wanted the best for me, but at that time it sure felt awkward. I ran into major adjustment issues, and one of the biggest was telling myself that I was too dumb to speak up and speak out. So, my actions gained all my attention when I acted out, got in trouble, and found myself in the principal's office on numerous occasions. At one point, I was even suspended. I kept an edge and flirted with being rebellious. By the time I reached the fourth grade, I figured out a new lie that I adopted as truth. I told myself that I did not belong at the school. Subconsciously, I had never, ever felt that I fit in.

One day, my teacher asked me to please come up to the front of the class and read a few lines from a book she had picked out for all the class to read. Other students had gone before me and had successfully accomplished their task. Now it was my turn! I slowly moved forward to the front of the class. It was at this moment that I noticed something very different about me. Out of the deep recesses of my inner self,

I heard a small, small voice. The voice was very subtle and non-threatening. It said, "You do not belong. You don't sound like the other children, and you are about to fail." Failing did not seem like an option—that is, it wasn't until I agreed with the inner voice I heard. I opened the book to the page my teacher had instructed me to read. I took a slow, long, deep breath and then exhaled. I looked up at my classmates and, for good measure, told myself I could do this. I could read. But for some apparent reason, it was too little, too late. The major damage of the Sniper had already occurred within my subconscious.

I started out strong, but after a few sentences I went downhill very fast. I ran into a few words I had trouble pronouncing. I started to stumble, and stammer, and stutter, and it began to happen. I lost my footing. I lost my place on the page. I started over. I became terrified. I was in trouble. Deep trouble. The only voice I heard was the toxic voice that told me I was a failure. Could it have gotten any worse? Yes! It got worse. What took place next was predictable and unthinkable. My fellow classmates began to snicker and laugh. How could this possibly be happening? It was as if, for some strange reason, I had invited everyone to Comedy Central or a comedy hour. My fears had come true! As I look back at this moment and other similar situations that unraveled in my life, it was not the fear that came true, but my words that aligned with the fears that became evident and true in my life.

> *What you say becomes true for you*
> *as you say it.*

I don't remember from where, but I have heard it said that if you say you can do something, the truth is you won't. However, if you say you are going to do a thing, the truth is you will. What you say becomes true for you as you say it and only as you say it. Other peoples' words are meaningless unless they become the truth for you. Words have power.

"I'm Out of Here!"

When I was growing up, the mentors in my family who served as examples to me were unpredictable, potentially dangerous, dicey and notorious, and they brought trouble by the nature of the games and arenas they played in. My family included known drug lords and drug dealers! In my first book, *Choices*, I talk about the rise and fall of my cousin, Tyrone Palmer (aka Mr. Millionaire), in the late 1960s and early 1970s. Despite the known fact that my cousin—"Fat Daddy" or "Ty," as we called him—was slain in Atlantic City at Club Harlem around Easter in 1974, my family still followed in his footsteps and became drug dealers. Stories abounded of countless family members becoming enslaved by narcotics, of family members being murdered, and of family members finally becoming victims of gang violence. These events came with the territory of being associated with the drug sales life.

Somehow, I was willing to venture down this same beaten path amid a plethora of circumstances involving the FBI, the CIA and the local police. I knew my doors could be kicked in by these and others, like the stick-up boys, the brody boys, the obsessed drug fiends who showed up at all hours of the night lurking, begging and trying to stick a pistol in my mouth so they could get their fix and take what they believed was rightfully theirs. The game itself was dangerous; yet, knowing that fact meant nothing to me as an adult. Family relationships were one aspect of the game; however, friendships from as far back as high school also challenged my ability to cope or make any kind of sensible choice.

While I was in high school, one of the greatest highlights of entering the weekend with my friends was either the Friday night dances or the house parties. I had a friend who played basketball for our school. Because he was my friend, my best friend, I got carte blanche and was taken along with him to certain functions. There was a particular day that one of the most popular girls in school, a cheerleader, was throwing a house party. Now, you need to understand that the house parties back in those days were thriving, and, when entering the house, you could feel the heat from all the people dancing downstairs. When we came into the girl's house, we all went down the steps toward the party. The heat intensified. The music was throbbing. We could literally feel the house shaking.

When we got downstairs, all the lights were off except for the black lights. Groups of individuals were standing along the wall. Other individuals were getting punch to drink. Others were speaking and talking in corners. And, of course, there was the dance floor. Now, prior to coming to the party, my boy and the others in the car all talked about getting phone numbers. In those days the idea was, if you went to a party, you had to come out with phone numbers. So, as I surveyed the situation and started to make my way to dance with a young lady, I watched some of the girls pursue my friend and the others with me. The party went on. The night was long. At the end, I came out with not one phone number. Although I asked, I did not get one phone number from any of the girls.

Before I realized it, the party was over, and I was the only one on the floor. Everyone else was heading upstairs. Soon, we all were heading out the door. Then all of us piled into a friend's car. Everyone except myself talked about how much fun they had and how the girls were all over them. They pulled out their phone numbers and started to count how many they had. I remained silent to avoid having to reveal the obvious. For some strange reason, my silence became an express telegram to everyone in the car that there was something wrong. I shrugged off the onslaught of questions until I could not take it anymore. My defense became the urge to fight. I wanted to lash out. In the past, those conversations I had with myself always came true. Then, out of the blue, I was sideswiped with a new thought. It said, "I'm out of here! Yes! I'm leaving. That's it. I will run from my apparent problem. I'm out!" And I did just that. Those words played over and over in my head until I believed what I had heard. "I'm out of here" was about to become my reality. I could no longer hear anything except, "I'm out of here." So, when my friend's car came to a stoplight, I bailed. I said to myself, "I'm out of here," and my actions followed. I opened the door, and my feet moved me away from the car. No one was expecting that. My actions were extreme. Once again, my thoughts became things. This single outburst caused a lot of friction with everyone except my boy Slick, who was my best friend. He rolled with it as if nothing was wrong. Later, this incident was swept under the rug with so many others because of our friendship; however, never without consequence. Unfortunately, the more I traveled down this path, the worse things got.

What follows all belief is action.

That same summer, another one of my friends, someone remarkably close, tried his hand at a bad joke. It was something very innocent, as I look back on it. It was along the lines of name-calling. Well, without warning, I received a thought from headquarters: my head, my inner voice. That voice said, "Smack the taste out of his mouth." And that is what I did. I heard that thought loud and clear, and within seconds my actions followed. I sized up the smaller stature of my friend and believed that not only could I hit him, but also that I could do it without repercussions. Or so I thought. The belief was there, and what follows all belief is action. I reached back and with one, long, hard swing from South Florida, I hit him upside his head. The look of surprise on his face is seared into my memory. His glasses hit the ground, and he collapsed as he clasped his face with both hands. I watched his eyes water up, but he said nothing, and neither did I. That relationship was never the same. I lost a dear friend. I gave no apology, and the friendship was severed. I often thought, after sizing him up, would my actions have been the same if he were like the great Mike Tyson? I won't waste anyone's time, or humor anyone, knowing we all know that answer.

Chapter Two

KEEP MOVING UNTIL YOU SEE THE LIGHT

"SUCCESS IS A JOURNEY, NOT A DESTINATION.
IT REQUIRES CONSTANT EFFORT,
VIGILANCE AND REEVALUATION."

———————

MARK TWAIN

This cosmic puzzle called life is one that we each must decipher and solve. No one else can arrange our pieces for us. Later in my life, as I worked hard to solve my life puzzle, I discovered within the depths of my imagination what it is I am supposed to be and contribute to the world. Nothing more; nothing less. Today I hold a set of keys and have used them to unlock the mysteries of my life, and I believe I am to share them so others may unlock their own. In short, I discovered who I am.

I believe, as we grow, we are exposed to more information in life. This information includes our education, experiences, mistakes, challenges—minor or great—even down to the most minute or seemingly trite incidents that occur. Every interaction and contact we have with every person we meet or encounter brings information. The answer to my question, "Who am I?" will change from time to time as I grow. It will not change drastically, but it will change. Here is one example.

Living the Dream

Let's look at the "perfect" family. We have "Elizabeth" and "Bill" who met in college and fell in love. Bill was a model student who, in his junior year, transferred from a local community college to Choice University and was now majoring in architectural engineering. Bill, the analytical type, fell head over heels for this young country girl, Elizabeth, who preferred to be called "Bethe." Bethe majored in interior design. She was an A-type person with a "let's get it done" approach to life. Things came into her to-do box and were done immediately. She and Bill first met at a frat party. That was all it took. Once their eyes locked on each other, it was game on; or, in this case, game over.

For the next few years, after graduation, they lived together and worked hard at their respective careers. Bethe developed her skills and knack for interior design and landed an awesome job with a real estate firm. Her coworkers learned to love and appreciate her talents. Bill, on the other hand, got a job with a local engineering firm. He worked his way up from the bottom to earn a good hourly wage. The two of them together were living the American dream. Working hard and establishing credit, they built their first home. It was a small, three-bedroom, two-bath, single-level home in the suburbs that Bill designed and Bethe decorated. The only thing missing was children.

When they started out, their goals were to graduate from college with their respective degrees, land jobs and spend time together. Life, however, has a funny way of showing up and helping us move in different directions. I have seen this happen in epic proportions. On March 13, 2020, we all witnessed our country shut down due to Covid-19. Millions of Americans had to relearn many aspects of living. The phrase, "Embrace change and pivot," was coined. So, once Bethe found out that she was pregnant, it was time to pivot. Unbeknownst to both Bill and Bethe, their world was about to turn upside down. They were asked to come in for what seemed like a routine ultrasound for Bethe. It was her first trimester, and the doctor ran some tests. The tests came back a little off, and when Bethe saw the doctor's face, she knew something was wrong. Bethe was told not to worry, but worry she did. She became obsessed with worry. All she could think about was what could go wrong. She could not take her mind off this thought: something was wrong. One day she woke up and realized she was spotting. Bethe had suffered a miscarriage. This event crushed her world. She was devastated and felt like a failure, as if she was to blame. Her mind ran with new thoughts that were also very toxic. She thought to herself, "I should have done this," or "I wish I had done that." "If only I could have done this or that differently," she told herself.

> *The answer to the question, "Who am I?"*
> *may change from time to time.*

Bill was incredibly supportive, but he felt helpless when he attempted to comfort the love of his life because she was not having it. She did not want to be held, and when he gave her space, she would ask him what was wrong. Bill then realized the bills were stacking up, so he worked extra hours, which created even more distance and stress between the two. He enjoyed work. It gave him a sense of satisfaction as well as peace, since it kept him away from what now was a negative Bethe. Early in their relationship they had thoughts of getting married and settling down, but those thoughts now became fleeting and seemed very much out of reach. Life had gotten away from them. What should Bill do?

Bill sought out counseling through a life coach. He then sold the idea of meeting with someone to Bethe. Bethe was reluctant at first but thought it would be wise to get help. So, Bill and Bethe met with their new life coach over a course of several months. They started out one on one with their coach. Later they joined forces and met together. It was during these meetings that Bill and Bethe learned to develop coping skills, new goals, new dreams and a reason for their lives. This reason morphed into a purpose for living and a "why" to move on with their lives. The only problem was, they were now moving in two totally different directions.

Encountering Polarity

It was explained to them that everything in life has a meaning and a purpose. It was certainly evident that this mishap and tragedy that had landed at Bill and Bethe's doorstep was not their fault. This truth became apparent to them both as they realized and understood the meaning of polarity, that everything has its opposites. If you have an up, there must be a down. If you have an in, there must be an out. If there is a left, look for the right. In the case of both Bill and Bethe, yes, something went wrong, and it seemed to be bad. Was it painful? Absolutely. And it took extreme courage on their part to get to a point where they could see the good in the situation.

So, with their loss, there came a gain—the gain of understanding themselves and what that meant for them individually. Their situation caused them both to look deep and long into what they wanted out of life.

Bill had discovered a joy in working long, hard hours. His boss quickly noticed his hard efforts. This certainly worked in Bill's behalf because those hours helped him to perfect his craft. He later became the lead go-to guy within the company. If something needed to be done, everyone went to Bill. He got so much recognition that when his boss decided to sell the company, he approached Bill, who bought the company and all its shares. Bill's hard work paid off. He now ran a multi-million-dollar engineering company that employed thousands of workers. His main mission statement said, "When in the dark, don't give up. Keep moving until you see the light."

Bill's business served millions of customers and clients all over the world. He was revered in his community and served on the boards of several foundations. A philanthropist at heart, he was always looking to give to the greater good. Bill, now married to Pat, has two children. They adopted three more children, for a total of five. They were all very successful with children of their own, making Bill and Pat grandparents of thirteen. Bill became a great husband, a wonderful father, a man's man in the community, and a renowned business leader admired around the world.

Everything in life has a meaning
and a purpose.

Bethe, on the other hand, found satisfaction through other means. Plagued with guilt from her loss and not knowing what to do next, she began to write and journal as instructed by her life coach. She felt comfort from writing. Writing became a relief, providing a sense of peace that allowed her to escape the guilt of her past.

Bethe's next steps were profound. It was explained to her that she might have been blessed with what seemed to be a curse: polarity! Her life coach pointed her in the direction of writing her own book. She thought this was a splendid idea, and she believed that she would in turn help others who had had similar experiences or whose situations were perhaps even worse. She was in the darkness and kept moving until she saw the light. Once the light switch turned on, it was game on, and she became like the old Bethe. She went to work with a new attitude and mission. She had rediscovered her new "why."

To date her books (yes, I said books) have sold over millions of copies and have been featured on talk shows and best-seller lists. She also regained her footing and found someone she loved. They married and raised a beautiful child who became a world-renowned pediatric doctor.

Life sure seems to have a way of unfolding very differently than it began. Both Bill and Bethe found their way and their why in life, and it was certainly different than when they started out.

My very trusted readers, as much as I would like to tell you this story is altogether true, it is not. Bits and pieces were taken from different life coaching experiences shared with my clients throughout the years. The story was created to prove a point and to shed some light on the topic of polarity. The next story is true, however. It is unequivocally, one hundred percent true. I can attest to that fact because the story is mine.

Chapter Three

THE ANSWER IS INSIDE

"IT IS NOT LIGHT THAT WE NEED, BUT FIRE; IT IS NOT THE GENTLE SHOWER, BUT THUNDER. WE NEED THE STORM, THE WHIRLWIND AND THE EARTHQUAKE."

FREDERICK DOUGLAS

Where do I begin? I would like to say it is safer to start at the beginning and throw open the front door, so to speak, but that is not as fun. So let's go in the back door of my path nearer the end.

A midlife crisis starts somewhere between forty and sixty years old. I was in my early forties. I was exhausted—exhausted to the point of giving up all hope of living. Fleeting thoughts of contemplating suicide raced through my mind, exiting as quickly as they had entered. I was afraid of ever actually committing such an act. However, if I was honest, the life I had chosen to live at that time certainly promoted death. I was faced with death daily. I was on a quest to either kill myself or allow someone else to do the job for me. As I said, I was exhausted.

I had tried all kinds of illicit drugs, including methamphetamine, crystal meth and heroin. I also had taken many kinds of prescription drugs like Vicodin, Dilaudid, Quaaludes, Valium, Percocet, Percodan, triple bar Xanax and other similar narcotics. This list does not include the other drugs I took, such as crack cocaine, powdered cocaine, marijuana and alcohol. Always alcohol. And more alcohol. To be sure, I was not a functioning addict; I constantly took these drugs every day, all day, as soon as I could get my hands on them. Most of the time I was under the influence of some type of substance. I was pretty much out of my mind twenty-four hours a day, seven days a week.

I recall one day when I was running a check scam. Understand, I did have a world-class coach and mentor who taught me the forgery game very well. But I also knew that anytime you mixed drugs and alcohol while attempting a constructive, or even unconstructive, act, you were going to fail. Your faculties leave you. Consequently, I was picked up by the Philadelphia police department on Ridge Avenue for this check scam. I was booked, fingerprinted and photographed as one of Philadelphia's finest. Next, I was transported to Montgomery County Correctional Facility, MCCF, where I faced open charges and probation violations. This is where my story really begins.

"Robber Gunned Down by Store Owner"
I rarely missed a meal when I was incarcerated, but, on this day, I slept through lunch. When I realized my predicament, I was very upset with myself and extremely hungry! I was angry as well. To make things worse, cold air from a vent overhead constantly blasted me while I slept in my new humble abode, my nine- by fourteen-foot, cold, clammy,

concrete cell. Momentarily having gained back my senses, I sat up slowly and planned my next move. My cellmate, whoever he was at the time, had gone to the day room with all the other men. Remember, this was not my first time throwing bricks at a prison, as the saying goes. It was not my first rodeo, in other words. I hopped off my bunk and walked to the day room, which was a sectioned-off pod. As I stepped onto the pod, I reached back with my arms, stretching them up in the air, and belted out a yawn. That stretch felt good. I was ready to face anyone or anything. (By the way, it is vital to keep moving in prison. If you lie around too much, your body becomes one with the environment, as stiff as the concrete blocks and steel bars surrounding you. On the outside I had usually slept off my stupors, but not in here! Not in prison. I had to keep moving at all costs to preserve my body and mind.)

As I moved toward a group of men positioned in a semi-circle around a twenty-inch television mounted on the wall, I noticed a few familiar faces. Jails, prisons and penitentiaries serve as revolving doors for those who want to return. Recidivism is real, and there is something to be said about the repeat offenders' club. Its members are non-judgmental. The only exception to this is the contempt for heinous crimes against children. Across the board, it is almost the cardinal rule. You harm children, and you get what you got coming to you.

I made eye contact with a few of the guys on the pod. We nodded our heads, looked at each other, and sauntered on. I asked what was on television and was told to keep my voice down. Obviously, these men did not know me, but their vibe seemed friendly enough, so I decided not to make any waves. Doing so would cause future trouble. That I knew for sure. Until you get the lay of the land in prison, it is best to keep to yourself. So, I did.

As I watched the television, the local news that was on was broadcasting something familiar. There had been a shooting. I was drawn to the story and focused deeply on the screen. A would-be robber had been gunned down by a store owner. Immediately, I was taken back in time as if it were made to stand still. It was as if some kind of magnetic pull had me in its grip. "Robber gunned down by store owner," the news anchor declared. Trancelike, I continued to stare at the television. This event felt so very real to me, but I had no idea why.

The would-be robber, now dead, had entered a local store in southwest Philadelphia. I leaned in closer, listening. I noticed the yellow cones around the dispersed gun shell casings on the ground. The crime scene was taped off, and people were in the background, most of them just hoping to be seen on television.

In the next moment, it was as if I had run one hundred miles per hour headfirst into a brick wall, and I realized in an instant why the story was familiar. I worked to push my way forward through the men clustered around the television to get a better view of the screen. The store owner's face was eerily familiar as he explained to the newscaster that he had been robbed a few weeks earlier and that this sort of thing was ruining his business. I realized then that I had stolen from this very same store owner two weeks before arriving at Montgomery County Correctional Facility, MCCF, my new residence.

Prior to my arrest, I was doing what I did best. I was in southwest Philly burning up every dollar I got my hands on and getting high with no rhyme or reason. Sometimes I didn't want to get high, but it had become a deeply embedded way of life and a habit I could not control. I would do just about anything to get a dollar to turn so I could shut down my reality because my reality was excruciatingly painful. It was painful, scary and so dark that I could not see any light. I wanted to end it all.

I would stay up for days on end, chasing the high I got from my favorite drug I nicknamed "Maggie May": crack cocaine. I romanticized my addiction by naming the drug after the popular 1971 hit song "Maggie May" performed by Rod Stewart. I didn't sleep, eat, wash my clothes or myself. Often, I would smell something bad, only to realize seconds later the odor was coming from me. Sometimes I did something about it, while other times I was too busy getting high and so ignored the reality of my own filthiness. My true reality lay stuck in this deep rut, this endless cycle of existence that I could not escape.

My personal crime sprees were beginning to get closer and closer to home. At first, I would travel out of the city and into the suburbs to commit crimes, but slowly and surely that circle grew smaller and smaller until wherever I landed, there I would show up. I stopped caring about how I lived and what I was doing. I lived with the mentality of a complete narcissist, sticking my chest out to the world and wearing what I considered an attitude badge across my chest reading "F--- it!" As if it meant something.

You did not want to be a friend of Ron James at this time in my life. Being a friend of Ron James meant someone was going to hunt you down for committing some type of wrongdoing or for having an unscrupulous association with me. It did not matter who I hurt, be it family, friends or even myself. Everyone was subject to my madness, my reality. But please ask yourself, what is reality? My definition boiled up from the depths of my imagination. My reality was life as I understood it.

Our answers are always inside of us.

As I recall, it was blazing hot outside; it was in the middle of summer when the sun sets late in the day. I felt desperate.

Confused. Broken. Life was not meant for me. I could not take hold of my creative mind and use it to discover the answers to my life problems. The answers slept deep inside, untouched. Undiscovered. Like a setting summer sun you know is there but rarely comprehend. In this state of mind, I had to figure out how to make some money. Certainly, there was always the conventional method of getting a job and working for an hourly wage, walking away with that weekly paycheck. But that meant cleaning up my act and presenting myself well in front of an employer, which nine times out of ten I did. I would sell myself well and get the job, only to end up right back at the beginning—or the end, depending on how you look at it. My desire to get money was driven by the passion of wanting to get high. I came up with many creative ways to do that. Creativity is an amazing thing!

Consequently, I established a creative cycle of raising capital. I found myself walking down the street on trash day, and a thought struck me. I could be a garbage man, of sorts. Not the typical garbage man you would see on your block, but one far different. I would take the can, get a bag out of it, and sort through the garbage looking for information such as discarded checkbooks, bank statements, credit card offers, old car titles or whatever had information. I found all kinds of important documents. I took all this information and used it as a starting point from which to build a profile. I worked the system using forgery, or someone else's identity, to create my own personal wealth. Sometimes I got as much as $10,000 in one day. But it always ended up in the same place. No matter how well I used my mind to get the money, it turned to ashes. I used it for drugs and unrighteous living. Plain and simple, my desire was not to obtain money. My desire was to burn it up by getting high.

If only I had used my creative mind for something positive. I knew that if I could stop long enough to allow my mind to focus on my desire, on getting what I wanted out of life, I could get it. The answers were always inside of me. Our answers are always inside of us. I told myself that I wanted to get high, and I moved in the direction toward fulfilling my wish. The next two stories show the opportunities I took to continue my narcissistic behavior without a second thought to anything or anyone else. I do not recommend or advocate this behavior.

Making a Plan

I recall that I had found some starter checks. Digging through a travel backpack in which I kept my belongings, I located one of these checks. My plan was to use it to purchase merchandise that I could later sell in exchange for drugs. It was not uncommon for me to take whatever I could get from any merchant store or business owner. I would buy alcohol, cigarettes, electronics, clothes, sneakers or food such as dry goods, produce or meat. If you had something to offer and your store was open for business, then you were fair game. Department stores, sporting goods stores, mom and pop shops, coffee shops and one of my favorites, the "jug," better known as the bank. I would make my way in the front door with a plan to walk out victorious. That was my philosophy, my mindset, even if I did not get anything! I was also a borderline kleptomaniac. If I could not buy something with a check, I would ask to use the bathroom at the back of the store, away from cameras, and help myself to whatever I could find. Then I would turn around and sell the merchandise to get what I really wanted. I took my booty, swag, goods or merchandise straight to anyone who was willing to purchase them—family, friends, strangers, someone on the side of the street, drug dealers or someone in a bar (a bar was a great place to drop off, unload and get rid of a lot). If anyone gave me a moment to tell what I was selling, someone was going to buy. It was just that simple.

Nighttime was quickly approaching, and my window of opportunity was closing fast. Many stores had already shut their doors to patrons. For me to pull off this scam correctly, I needed to clean up my act and look the part. With hair growing out of every part of my face, I looked disheveled, to say the least. I ended up going into one of the local crack houses and promising the owner that if he would work with me and allow me to wash up, I would reward him. He agreed with no questions asked. He must have known that every time I came there, I was loaded down with all kinds of merchandise, and, if not, I had something to offer in the form of drugs. I was still half lit and had many drugs in my system. However, I could still perform under the influence of most drugs. My one nemesis was alcohol. Alcohol did something to me that took me completely over the edge. Either my words would slur or I would walk sideways. My head would be cocked in a direction that spelled disaster. I am certain others could tell something was wrong with me when I was drunk.

I could reverse this effect by using meth, a line of coke or crack cocaine. Then I would be back at the top of my game. Of course, the cycle would always repeat itself. That was a bigger problem. If I had some cocaine to level myself out, there was no need for me to leave. But then I would be stuck, so it was off to the races again.

I needed a car to get me to a shopping center or an outlet mall because the stores were closing soon. It became the only problem in my mind. That, and remembering which stores I could not return to, ones that I had already hit, which could result in a fast track back to prison. You would think this would not be a big deal, that you would remember where you went and who you stole from. In my case, I always had some type of substance in my system, so I was liable to make a lot of mistakes no matter how good I thought I was.

In major cities across the country like Philly, there were individuals who would drive their personal cars just like a taxi service. Today they are known as Uber drivers; back then they were called hacks. The odds were against me. I did not have any money for a hack. Nor did I have any supporting ID for what I needed to pull off in my check scam. Things were looking grim; it looked like I lacked what I needed to bring the scam to fruition. However, what I did have was desire. I had a determination like no other, and that determination was not going to be squandered. It took all my mental resources to pull off what happened next, since I was not about to give up. As a matter of fact, I was just getting started.

"It's a Visa Check"
With no vehicle, no form of transportation, and no backup ID; with stores closing for the night; and with no money to get high, most people would call it a night and think that tomorrow is another day. That sounds like a good excuse for someone willing to give up or take a break. Taking a break, though, is not in my DNA. If I can see it, I can say it. If I can say it, I'm speaking it, and it is going to come to be.

> *If I can see it, I can say it. If I can say it,*
> *I'm speaking it, and it is going to come to be.*

It was time to get creative. I took a blank starter check out of my backpack and held it up to the light. I thought to myself, "What could this really be if I put my mind to it?" The answer was astonishing. I envisioned this seemingly worthless piece of paper as a Visa check. I pulled out my trusty black pen and wrote $100 in the memo section of the "Visa check," then made up a fictitious Visa number starting with 4XXX and wrote it and the words VISA CHECK on it. This bold and brazen act created all kinds of finances for me that were unexplainable. Next, I headed on foot to the part of town where I could catch a hack and talk him into taking me shopping. He would wait for me, and I would pay him with some of the proceeds from my shopping spree. However, I soon ran into another challenge. There were absolutely no hacks available, and it appeared as if my plan were coming to a screeching halt. I began to walk and walk and walk. As I thought on what to do next, I looked up and right in front of me was my answer. On the street corner ahead of me in Southwest Philadelphia was a store—a corner bodega.

I walked up these ragged, broken-up cement steps leading into the store. I grabbed the doorknob and turned it slightly, then I walked in. As I did so, to my astonishment I heard something unfamiliar. A store like this bodega in my area would not have had this type of sound. I heard tinkling bells like you might hear when entering an old store in the South. It was obvious the bells were meant to alert the store owner that someone was entering the store. Then the ringing stopped abruptly, and I was greeted with another sound. It was the voice of the store owner approaching me and letting me know he was in charge and someone in authority. This five-foot, five-inch slender Asian man belted out in a deep voice with broken English, "How may I help you?" I quickly turned on my charm. I wanted to blow him away with a smile and win him over with my schoolboyish mannerisms. Things seemed to be working in my favor instantly. I noticed his body language had melted into a calm state, and the two of us began to openly communicate with a mutual degree of respect. I told him I was having a spectacular day and was there to pick up a few things for me and my family members whom I said were waiting for me. This of course was a bold-faced lie, but I was trying every tactic I could to convince him I was there for the right reasons.

In the meantime, I circled in and around the store aisles, grabbing things I thought would be easy to sell. I tried to give off the impression that I was having a party, so I grabbed napkins, paper plates, chips, soda and anything else to convince him. I was hoping to run up the bill to as close to sixty dollars as possible with the intention of getting him to cash the "traveler's check" and hand me the forty dollars in change, which, of course, I was going to use to get high. But something went terribly wrong. It was as if he had seen a ghost. He seemed to become alerted to the fact that this was none other than a full-fledged scam in progress. He stopped dead in his tracks, lifted his head as he was preparing a sandwich I had ordered for the party, and said to me, "You pay first." I quickly agreed with a pleasant gesture. Without losing any of my composure, I headed to the counter, reached into my pocket, and pulled out the check. I simply looked at it first and then handed it to him without a flinch.

I could tell the store owner was confused. He looked at the check for about five or six seconds. It seemed like an eternity, however, before he responded. The bewildered look on his face said it all. He blurted out, "What is this?" I calmly stated, "Oh, it's a Visa check." His voice went up about twenty notches, and I witnessed a true transformation of his body language. His eyebrows turned in, he breathed heavily, fire appeared in his eyes, and his face flushed. I knew he was preparing to say something I didn't want to hear. I remained very relaxed and thought to myself, "Wait for it." I repeated it again to myself, "Wait for it." I knew something was coming, and on cue he yelled out, "We no take checks." After he repeated this to me several times, I said to the man, "Please, take it easy." I dropped my voice to a slow, calm tone and said, "No worries. Sir, let me run to the MAC machine and get some cash." I had no MAC machine (better known as an ATM machine today) to go to. I did not even have a credit card or bank card. This meant no money, no goods and no drugs to get high on.

As my check scam did not work out, I quickly moved to Plan B. Let me tell you that, although it didn't work that day, I soon perfected my "Visa check scam" to the tune of thousands of dollars on any given day. I am not bragging or glorifying my wrongdoing, only highlighting mindful creativity. I believed in myself and used my creative mind along with determination to get what I wanted. Doing things repeatedly until they were perfected could be called genius. I just truly believe that if we can see something, we can bring it to pass.

On my way out of the store, I noticed a display of Pampers. Yes, disposable diapers were next to the door. I rushed to the display and kicked it toward the door. It was in a blind spot for the store owner, and I took advantage of it. As I reassured him of my return, I quickly bent over and grabbed some Pampers and slipped out the door. As I made my escape in stealth mode, I heard the familiar bells tinkling again behind me. This could only mean one of two things. Either someone had entered the store after I came out—which was not the case—or the store owner was in hot pursuit of the Pampers and me!

Drugs, alcohol and any poor choices I made were not the issue. My issue was me! I wanted what I wanted, and I was willing to sacrifice anything to get it. My desire was so strong that I put my life on the line for a pack of Pampers.

I slowly turned my head to glance in the direction of the sound of the tinkling bells. I decided that if he yelled at me again, I would just take off running and slip into the night. However, sometimes the best, or worst, plans can trip up anyone. That was certainly the case that night. Things were about to get crazy real fast. I spotted him about ten yards behind me. He yelled at the top of his lungs in his native language. He was telling me to stop. Well, in my language "stop!" means "go," and go as fast as you can! As I ran, I noticed something wasn't normal about this situation. "What was wrong," I thought as I looked back. It instantly became clear that as he raised his hands, they came together clasping and clutching a gun. I spun back around toward the direction I had been running and kicked it into high gear. I felt a rushing wind swish past my left ear. This was followed by the sound of clapping, or gunfire. My body tensed up as I looked for cover and dipped in and out of the cars parked along the street. I somehow made my way to an alley at the end of the block and ran down it, disappearing into the night at last.

Chapter Four

WHO, WHERE, WHY

"WHAT YOU CAN'T IMAGINE, YOU CAN'T DISCOVER."

———————————

ALBERT EINSTEIN

I got away, or so I thought. You know, it is funny how we never get away with just anything. Somehow, no matter where I went, I ended up with consequences, despite how hard I tried to do things differently. My best and worst self showed its ugly face, and there I was in prison.

I was standing in a trance amongst other inmates. The hairs on both my arms and my back were standing up. I learned from the news report on the television that the person who robbed the store after me did not make out so well. In an awkward way, I realized for the first time that it could have been me instead of him. The bullets that left the chamber of the store owner's gun had a name on them, but it wasn't mine that day. It was not my time to go, but my world was crashing in on me with incredible force regardless. I began to think long and hard about why I was even still here and why it hadn't been my time to go. I could not come up with an answer, and eventually I came up with another question instead: "Where was I going?" That question then led me to yet another question, one that struck at the very core of my being: "Who am I?" It took me several years and several trips back and forth to prison to finally find the answers to those three simple questions. "Why was I here?" "Where was I going?" "Who am I?"

Free in Prison

I spent twenty-five years doing the same things over and over and getting the same results before a light bulb moment, an epiphany, took place, shining a light on a way out. It goes like this: "Where your mind goes, your energy flows." Your thoughts become your reality. Your ideas become real to you. Those things that you believe to be true are true for you. My life changed the moment I saw myself doing something differently! I began to speak life into my present situation. As a matter of fact, I have always spoken life into my present situation, even though the words, the ideas, were destructive and chaotic, filled with doubt, fear and torment. Those ideas became my reality and manifested themselves in my beliefs.

There is an old saying that when the student is ready, the teacher will appear.[3] Well, my teachers came rushing in from all directions. I began to see life from a different perspective. I learned from programs. I learned from reading books and quotes and from listening to mentors and even other inmates, some of whom as "lifers" will never go home. Old friends, new friends and some enemies showed up, leading me and pointing me in safe directions. What was so strange

---

3 Some attribute this saying to Lao Tzu, but that is apparently not substantiated.

was that I could now see life differently, as though through a new pair of lenses. Even nature seemed different. I was in a new world I had never seen before. I had a new perspective! It seemed to me I had become unstoppable. Any positive thought, saying, quote, affirmation or word of encouragement began to inspire me and lead me in a very compelling way. I was on fire. By opening my cell door to new ideas, I became active in my own release. I had thrown myself a lifeline of hope and did not even realize it. No longer did I believe that I could not do something. Now I knew I could do it, and I would do it. This time, however, I wanted to get it done in a positive way.

I was free. *Yes, it was in prison that I became free.* Time was no longer against me; time was finally on my side. Millions of people today walk around in some kind of bondage. They are locked up in their self-made prison constructed brick by brick by themselves.

> *By opening my cell door to new ideas,*
> *I became active in my own release.*

I know some of you are thinking about the situation that happened to me when I was young. That situation was one I had no control over. "What about that?" you ask. I can safely say that there are no absolutes. It's kind of an oxymoron, right? That, in and of itself, is absolute. I like to position it this way: At some point in our lives, when we come to an understanding of who we are, where we are going, and why we are here, we will be released from all resentments, hatred and things that hold us in bondage. Instead of looking at a situation that was ugly, I take it and love on it, embracing the fact that it happened for a reason. It is for that reason you can release that energy for the good of those around you and for the sole purpose of freeing yourself.

This concept may sound crazy to some of you; however, I can share firsthand that once I was able to embrace the fact that I was who I was, it released me into who I wanted to be. I now embrace the fact that I went to prison. I embrace the fact that I was a drug addict. I embrace the fact that I lived homeless. I embrace the fact that I lived "less than" and hurt people. In doing so, I can help a multitude of others avoid going down the same paths I went down, possibly to receive the same things I received or even worse. I no longer believe that I am any of those negative things. I now see myself for who I say that I am, and that "I am" is created out of my own imagination.

The most important thing we all have going for us is our imagination. We operate out of the idea that either we can or we can't. We are either in faith or we are in fear. We cannot have it both ways. Once we come to the realization that we cannot live out of both spectrums, we are faced with the harsh reality of making a choice. I say, choose faith. Choose being positive. Choose to believe that you can. At the end of the day, no matter what you choose, it will be your choice and your reality. You say that you want to change. Well, whose dream is it to change? If you listen to the discouraging voices of your past, your parents, your neighbors or your so-called friends that it won't work, then it can't work. "You are too small, too fat, too ugly, too light, too dark, too young or too old. You are a failure like your dad or your mom. Why would anyone choose you? You are going to end up in jail. It's not the right time for you. It never worked for me; it's impossible for you. It's impossible for that to happen. It's impossible." One of the greatest things I've ever heard someone do or suggest is this: Go get your dictionary and cut out the word *impossible*. (Napoleon Hill, author of *Think and Grow Rich*, said one of the first things he did when he purchased a dictionary—this was in 1937—was look up the word *impossible* and neatly cut it out of the dictionary so it would no longer be a part of his vocabulary.) An infinite list could be written of every negative statement known to man. The most damaging aspect is that people will blindly believe these negative statements that others make to be true about themselves. When you adopt those sayings, they become your reality. It is then that you are living someone else's dreams. The idea that someone can prophesy over you and influence your life is impossible unless you take on the characteristic of believing those words.

From birth, we gain all kinds of insights, experiences, traditions, knowledge, ideas and suggestions from others. It is not until we come into a direct encounter with our self and tap into our own imagination that we connect with God, the universe and others.

Fortunately, after several decades of poor choices, I have come to the illuminating reality that my life has meaning. That meaning, which I live out of my own God-given imagination, is to equip and empower each person I encounter to help that person find his or her own meaning. My purpose is to help anyone I meet become the best version of self he or she can be. I choose now to live my life helping others see the full potential of their expectations and existence.

As I reflect on my life, I think part of my problem was I did not know what I did not know. Thus, two very important questions immediately take up residence in my spirit. The first question is, "What is it that I do know?" The second question is, "What is it that I do not know?"

I will take a stab at answering both questions in a moment, but first I want to throw in a third question: "How much of what you think you know do you really know?" And does "what you think you know" fall under your own reality or under the perception of others? What is reality? My definition happens to be life as I understand it. No more; no less.

Everything I perceive as being true or false simply comes from the imagination. This could be from my imagination or the interpretation of others' imaginations if I choose to believe what others say is true. Everything I have received as being true or false has come off the heels of mankind's thinking from generation to generation as far back as man has existed. Just ask yourself, "Why do I do the things that I do? Did I learn them from a self-help book, or did my parents teach me what I know? Or was it a friend or colleague?" Whatever the case, you were moved, inspired or enlightened by someone or something that wired you to believe the way you believe. So now you believe. Here is a simple explanation from a story I once heard. Like my earlier story about Bill and Bethe, even though it is fictional, it has meaning and impact and proves a point.

"Why?"

There was an amazing blended American family that, if you were to trace their roots, you would find they came from all over the world. They were of Irish, Asian, French, African and Native American descent. The family was a true melting pot and representation of what America is today. This family came together every year to participate in one of the greatest American holiday practices: Thanksgiving. Originally from the deep South, the Anderson family, when it came to Thanksgiving, knew how to celebrate. They could throw down when it came to cooking. They were a class act second to none. What did the Andersons serve up for Thanksgiving? Like every American family, Thanksgiving meant turkey. However, the Andersons had a special roasted turkey with a special cream-style stuffing along with a second turkey that was deep fried. When you cut into the turkeys, the meat was so tender you could see the moisture dripping from it. Next, there were candied yams, buttered rolls, homemade cornbread and deep-dish macaroni and cheese with six kinds of cheeses. There were green beans, collard greens, fried fish, okra, baked beans with ham, and cranberry sauce, not to mention all the desserts like apple pie, pecan pie, sweet potato pie, peach cobbler, cookies, fudge and pound cake. Then there was also the family's staple dish, which was Great-Great-Grandmother's succulent roast recipe. This recipe was handed down from generation to generation. Precisely prepared to perfection, the roast was always the first dish on the table to disappear, and everyone's plate included slices of it!

Louise Anderson was a bright, proud, charismatic and very inquisitive seven-and-a-half-year-old little girl. Whenever she was asked her age, she made sure "and a half" was included or there would certainly be trouble. It was the morning of Thanksgiving Day, and Louise had wandered into the kitchen. She was enthralled as she watched her mother orchestrate every area of the kitchen and, wanting to help, offered her assistance. Her mother thought this would be a great opportunity to share some of the family traditions with her daughter and welcomed the opportunity. The mother continued working on the roast, seasoning it to perfection. She cut both ends off the roast and placed it in the pan, then tossed away the roast ends. Louise sat back with a look of curiosity. Mom Anderson knew the look all too well and waited for the question to follow. Louise did not disappoint. She blurted out, "Mom, why did you cut the ends off a perfectly good roast?" Mom Anderson gathered her thoughts and responded, "This is how we have always done it." Keep in mind that just because something is always done a certain way, does not make it right. Nor does it mean that it always must remain that way. Remember, we don't know what we don't know.

Louise continued her line of questioning. Mom Anderson finally came up with an answer she did not want to give, but it was truly an honest answer. She said, "I honestly don't know." She then went on to say that Grandma would be over that day, and they could ask her. Both Mom Anderson and Louise were relieved, knowing they could get to the bottom of this mystery of the roast without ends.

Later that evening in a crowded room over dinner, Louise posed the question to "Mimi," her grandmother. All were surprised when Mimi said that, unfortunately, she did not know the answer to the profound question. The mood at the table then changed because everyone could see the disappointment on Louise's face. She immediately said, "Okay, I understand," and she let it go.

Several months later, Louise accompanied Mimi and Mom Anderson to the nursing home to visit her elderly Great-Grandmother, who was failing in health. Louise quickly took advantage of the opportunity to find an answer to her question about the roast without ends. "Grandmama, could you please tell me why Mom and Grandma Mimi cut the ends off the perfectly good roast at Thanksgiving?" Without hesitation, her great-grandmother delivered the answer. "Louise, that is a very good question, and I have a simple explanation for you. When I was a child like you, our family was very poor. My mother only had one pan to cook all the meals out of. So, when she made the roast, she would cut the ends off so it would fit into the pan." We don't know what we don't know!

So, there you have it. Both ends of the roast were cut to make it fit in the pan. This time-honored tradition was formed out of necessity. That one small but significant act became one the Anderson family did solely for tradition's sake. It was not right or wrong, but habitual. Please ask yourself this question. "How much of what I do was formed by habit or as a result of someone's truth, belief or reality that, to this day, continues affecting events and actions in my life?"

I have learned to challenge myself by asking a hard question: "If I continue doing this or that, will it or will I change?" My short answer is that my own insanity will come true; that I will know the end, and it will never change. But I don't know what I don't know. Or do I?

We don't know what we don't know.

Let's examine the question, "What don't I know?" How much of what you know, do you really know? Is it ten, twenty or fifty percent of everything there is to know about life? How much of that percentage have you mastered for your own understanding? Does a person's age have anything to do with the knowledge that individual acquired? Let me digress for a moment to touch on this point. I have three very bright, inspiring, intellectual, intelligent and amazing daughters. The first is Karissa, the second is Lanaya, and the third is Mireya. Their ages vary over a span of seventeen years. All of them have pushed, tested and challenged my intellect. As a parent, I think I always know what is best. Well, that is until I need their help. Take my youngest, who as of this writing is eight years old. (We can't forget that half.) She has the innate ability to figure things out. She can toggle through a cell phone like nobody's business and often helps me. So, with certain things, age has no meaning at all. At best, if I am honest, age matters less than a fraction of one percent. Let me elaborate. Take the word *all*, for instance. Does *all* really mean *all*? Is all-inclusive the sum of the entire matter? Now put *all* into a pie chart and fill it with all meaning and all things pertaining to life—every topic, every subject, every issue, every cause and effect—everything.

A few things to put in this pie chart come to mind: quantum physics, metaphysics and mathematics and its theories, including algebra, geometry, calculus combinations, complex analysis, constants and numerical sequences. There are also differentials, equations, elliptic functions, Euclidean and non-Euclidean geometry, Fourier series, history, logic, philosophy, mathematical physics, numbers, theory, probability, quotations, measurements, Boolean algebra…and the list goes on and on. What about astrology, human anatomy, science, the sea, how the eye works, the brain and its functions, and the conscious and the subconscious? I am sure you get my point. If not, let me continue. What is it that you don't know that has not been revealed yet? This question would be the same as, "What don't I know?" Now you have been brought full circle.

My life did not, nor could it, have come into fruition until I decided to throw myself a lifeline and then move out of my own way. I had to learn that I was not the one in control of my life despite having full control of my choices. My thoughts and self-talk were what became my reality. It did not matter what someone else said or what their opinions were. What mattered was what was real to me. Who was I? I was a manifestation of what I said I was and, consequently, who I became based on my true actions. I lied because I wanted to. I stole property because I wanted to. I smoked crack cocaine, drank and did all forms of prescription medications not prescribed by a physician solely because I wanted to. I lived homeless on the streets, ate very little or ate too much, cursed at people and put on a mask to hide my true feelings simply because I said that is what I wanted to do. At every turn, I took advantage of the people I lied to and manipulated. I chose to do whatever I told myself to do. When my inner voice encouraged me to do it, I did it. I listened and followed directions based on what I told myself. It was not until I spoke differently to myself that I began to change.

I would like to take a moment here to explain my take on choice in addiction.

I don't want to sound condescending, but I believe addiction is a personal choice. If you chose to use drugs or alcohol, then you must now live with that decision. It is not my intention to hurt anyone's feelings, but it's crucial to understand that it was *your* choice to introduce substances into your body, whether it was drugs or alcohol or another distraction you deemed more important at the time. Choices matter, and I emphasize that *choices are everything.*

The statement "choices are everything" isn't necessarily profound; it simply means that you made a choice and now it's up to you to make a different one, especially if your actions harm your family, friends or society.

Why does this matter? You picked up this book, seeking something that might inspire you to become a better person. Maybe the title intrigued you or the cover caught your eye, making you think it could help you.

Regardless of the reason you picked up the book, it's here to assist you in making new choices.

I might come across as firm, but I'm not sharing these lessons based solely on book knowledge (although I have read various books over the years that have influenced me positively, and I acknowledge them in this book). I don't claim any special credentials; instead, I rely on practical knowledge, echoing the advice of my mentor, Rob Jolles, a notable author, motivational speaker and coach.

In summary, I'm an expert based on my experiences, not on letters behind my name.

As a motivational speaker, published author and life coach myself, I have the privilege of traversing our nation, visiting various institutions such as schools, businesses, colleges, universities, juvenile detentions, prisons, churches, treatment facilities, therapeutic communities, rehabilitation centers and more. Within these diverse settings, I am afforded the opportunity to impart my story and message centered around the transformative power of choices.

My personal journey involved a pivotal shift from a narcissistic mindset fueled by self-service and the consumption of substances like alcohol, heroin, crack cocaine, prescription medications and marijuana and even addictive behaviors like overeating. This shift became a lifeline. It was like a sturdy stool with four essential legs, each crucial in supporting the whole. These four essentials are as follows:

1. Stop/Interpret

The first leg of this transformative stool involves the crucial step of stopping and interpreting one's situation. It's about acknowledging the need for change and understanding the impact of current behaviors.

2. Educate/See Yourself as You Are and Where You Want to Be

The second leg emphasizes education. It's about gaining awareness of one's self, recognizing the present state, and envisioning a desired future. Education becomes a mirror reflecting both the reality and the potential for personal growth. This is coupled with seeing yourself as you really are.

3. Create New Habits

Building on this foundation, the third leg advocates for the creation of new habits. It's the intentional cultivation of positive behaviors, steering one's self away from destructive patterns, and embracing routines that contribute to personal well-being.

4. Help Others

The final leg of this transformative stool is rooted in the principle of helping others. Extending a hand to those on a similar journey not only reinforces one's commitment to change but also contributes to a broader positive impact on the community.

Just as a well-balanced stool stands firm on its four legs, my theory on overcoming addiction aligns with these practical principles. This approach is not just a personal philosophy but a road map for all who seek positive transformation in their lives.

Chapter Five

SPEAK AND SEE

"IF YOU WANT TO CHANGE THE FUTURE,
YOU MUST CHANGE WHAT YOU ARE DOING
IN THE PRESENT."

―――――――

MARK TWAIN

How does one change? This incredible question has been around for ages and has a simple answer. You change using your imagination coupled with your faith. You change only when you see yourself for who you really are and who you really want to become. It is seriously as simple as that. My problem was not anything outside of me; my problem was me and how I saw myself.

How I saw myself was based on someone else's imagination of me and what I adopted, embraced or took on as my real self. It was based on the imagination I created out of my own mind. I took what others wanted me to be and became it. I was who I said I was only because I had built my life in the footsteps of others. I had never looked inward to have a deep, meaningful conversation with myself.

It was within myself where I finally saw me. And when I saw me, I realized that I did not like the man I had become. Once I realized all that I had become was built from others' imaginations, I began working backward to unravel the many presuppositions of my false realities. I faced my fears, my guilt, my resentments and my errant desires. I began to rethink myself by taking baby steps. These baby steps were essential to imagining and creating the person I wanted to become. I desperately wanted to be that man whom people looked up to. I wanted to be Ron L. James, a man willing to sacrifice it all to help others avoid ending up in a dark place like mine. I did not want people to feel "less than" or guilty.

For most of us, when we first get into trouble, it starts out small, like a scolding. The scolding is taken to heart. Little by little, more of life's messages become ingrained as negative and hurtful. We react in kind, and, before long, the results can include detention and/or suspension in school, expulsion, being fired, jailed, imprisoned in a penitentiary, homeless and addicted, whether to drugs, sex, alcohol, gambling or even working excessively. The pain of our addictions never gets better until a new choice is made. In fact, all poor choices take us down a road we do not want to travel.

I imagined and saw a new me, and faith brought it to pass. Now I can live in the imagination I saw.

Faith makes us sure of what we hope for and gives us proof of what we cannot see. (Hebrews 11:1 CEV®)

Understand that what I share here will help you only if you first find out who you are by looking long and hard into the mirror. You could study your reflection in the bathroom mirror, a pond or somewhere you can see yourself. Do it not for my sake, but for yours. If that is not something you can do, then I say close your eyes and use your imagination to do it. Look at yourself long, hard and deep. Once you have discovered all the things you don't like about yourself and the things you want to improve upon, then see those things anew.

How can you do this? I will give you two keys to successfully help yourself accomplish this task and bring your new view into fruition. Make the choice to truly see yourself for the first time.

What I share here are keys to success. I have used them and found the effects monumental. (To find out some of the other things I have done, read my book, *A Year of Choice, A Year of Change: Success Made Easy Through Monthly, Weekly, and Daily Practices.*)

"I Am Blessed"

As a motivational speaker who travels the country speaking to youth at schools and universities and even people in businesses, my message on choices is always the same. You have the choice to use your voice. Believe, and what you believe becomes reality. You can speak life to yourself by utilizing what I believe is the most powerful tool: affirmations!

You may already know or believe that you know about affirmations. You may even get ahead of me and say, "Don't you mean positive information?" Well, yes! And no! I say "no" because right, wrong or indifferent, whatever you say to yourself rings true. Simply put, if you say it, it is because you see it. If you see it, it is because you have spoken it. If you speak it, it is because you believe it. It is humanly impossible to have a belief system without an action associated or attached to it. So, if you say you can, or if you say you cannot, you are absolutely one hundred percent correct!

*You have the choice
to use your voice.*

As I learned how to read while incarcerated, I began reading self-help books—which is another key to success. It was within the pages of these books that I ran across quotes, statements and phrases, some of which spoke volumes. Statements such as, "I am who I say I am"; "I am amazing"; and countless others, I devoured. I began to meditate on them by repeating the positive information repeatedly until it brought life within my being. What was profound was that a lot of these sayings were handed to me countless times over the years as I grew up, but they held no meaning at the time. The seeds certainly were planted, but they did not take root until I started saying them to myself, until I was ready to receive them. Remember, "When the student is ready, the teacher will appear."

At this stage of change, you must start with what I call "humble beginnings." I would say that if you are reading this book, then you are at that point. You want to throw yourself a lifeline. If you are not at this point, let me share this thought. You can begin this positive process at any age, at any time or at any place in your life. Of course, the earlier you start, the better. That is why my wife and I have been using this tool with our daughter since she was four years of age.

Each morning before she brushes her teeth and each night before she goes to bed, she recites the following:

I am amazing.
I am incredible.

I am gifted.
I am loved.
I get better and better every day in every way.
Quitters never win, and winners never quit.
I am full of truth and wisdom.
I am blessed.

We have her make these statements solely to empower her and help her identify who she is. As she gets older, she will form her own positive affirmations to empower herself. I believe it is a never-ending process, one that she and you will always be able to continue by adding new insights as you grow and run into new challenges. Forming new positive affirmations will revolutionize your life.

As I travel the country speaking to students at universities and young men and women in juvenile detention centers as well as in juvenile prisons, I see the harm caused by negative words, words that can create an everlasting, devastating effect. It happened to me in my life.

Let's take a look at a simple exercise. How many of you have heard the following negative affirmations as you were growing up?

You are an idiot.
You are clumsy.
You are worthless.
Shut up.
I wish you were never born.
Do not speak unless you are spoken to.
You are fat.
You are ugly.
You are too small/too tall.
You are too dark/too light.
You are never going to make it.
You are a loser.

You are stupid.
You are going to jail.
You are going to die in the streets.

There is no humanly possible way to come up with every negative affirmation said to mankind, so I am going to ask you to fill in the blanks below with the words that have been haunting you for a lifetime, whether or not they were in the list you just read. Leave the "I AM" blanks empty for now.

You are _________________.   I AM _________________.

You are _________________.   I AM _________________.

You are _________________.   I AM _________________.

You are _________________.   I AM _________________.

You are _________________.   I AM _________________.

You are _________________.   I AM _________________.

You are _________________.   I AM _________________.

You are _________________.   I AM _________________.

You are _________________.   I AM _________________.

You are _________________.   I AM _________________.

You are _________________.   I AM _________________.

You are _________________.   I AM _________________.

Now draw a line through each phrase you wrote down. In the space after "I AM," add your own positive affirmation. Make sure these are positive affirmations.

This exercise will revolutionize your thinking, changing you from who you were into who you are. The many negative words directed at you over your lifetime have all been bold-faced lies. Yes, they were one hundred percent lies! The *only* way these lies become truth is if you and your imagination give them life by believing them. Your thoughts will become your truth if you choose to believe them. Speak positive truths so that you can live a new life free from the bondage and burden of guilt and toxic shame that someone else planted in your mind and heart. The opinions of others became what you believed, and they took root in your subconscious mind and vulnerable heart.

After you have identified the injurious words and crossed them out, see, say and speak your newly written, personal, life-giving and loving affirmations. *See it! Say it! Speak it! Believe and be it!*

This process *will breathe life into your very being.* You can use a mirror to aid you in the process. Use that mirror not only to see your reflection, but also to see yourself while speaking to yourself and doing the exercise using your own positive affirmations.

Envision It!

Another powerful tool will help you not only to simply use your imagination but also use it creatively. That tool is a vision board. What is a vision board? It is a collection of images and words that represent a true reflection of a person's heart, desires, goals, wants and wishes. A vision board will inspire and motivate you to visualize what has crossed the imagination of your mind.

Here are three simple ways to formulate your vision board. First, sit down with a piece of paper, poster board, or even a wooden board. Relax in a calm state of mind. I like to stare at empty space for some time to help me get clarity. Look deeply within yourself. The more relaxed you are, the better clarity and control you will have of the images that rush into your mind. Sometimes my thoughts are slow and precise, while other times it is like I am holding a teacup trying to catch water flowing from Niagara Falls! Then write your thoughts down. I always have fun brainstorming and allowing my imagination to run wild! I encourage you to take your time and do the same. Get busy and allow your imagination to expand.

Next, associate those images with a word or picture. For example, if you see yourself vacationing on an Alaskan cruise, reach for a book or travel magazine or even a newspaper where you saw a word or image related to an Alaskan cruise. Try to locate that word or picture, then cut it out. Attach this word or image on your paper, poster board, wooden board or even the wall in your office. Wherever you put it, that is your vision board. It will directly reflect the positive images you created and will soon manifest into your reality. Repeat the process with the next item on your list, searching for an image that works best for you. You may find yourself with one or more "visions" on your vision board. There are no rules as to how many images you choose to reflect yourself. Remember, you are doing this to inspire yourself!

I do have a word of caution, though. Your board is *your* board. It is not meant to be paraded around or prove anything to anyone other than yourself. It should not be worn as a badge of honor unless you are ready to defend it and talk about it. Take, for example, people who wear sports franchise images. They wear an image because they like and support its meaning. They are more than ready to defend their chosen image, if asked. So, if you are going to put your board out there for others to see, make sure you really want to do it. I recommend protecting your newly discovered words and images that came from your heart until you are ready to talk about them.

I created my first vision board while I was incarcerated. I hung that precious board on the wall in my cell. Every morning I would muse wide-eyed about the words and images, hoping beyond hope that my thoughts would become true. I would do the same every night before bed.

You can only imagine, as I sat in my cell creating my vision board, that one of my words started with the letter F. This "F" was extremely important to me. It stood for *freedom*. And it meant not simply freedom from incarceration, but freedom from the bondage in which I was living.

It is vital that you find a safe place where you can go daily and reflect on your vision board. As I mentioned earlier, share it only with trusted individuals. No one can see what you can see. Your vision board is best for your eyes only. Your vision board will come from *your* imagination. You have no need of continuing to live out others' imaginations for yourself. Others' inquisitions, sarcasm, criticism or even just their idea of what you should be is not what *your* vision board should reflect. If someone has a positive suggestion or a word of encouragement, that is always welcomed. However, you should still be cautious. Even if someone's feedback is from a place of good intention, people tend to inadvertently sabotage or rain on your parade. So, if you share your vision board, be ready for others' opinions. The bottom line, though, is that it is *your* vision board for *your* growth, not theirs.

Refer to and look at your board as often as possible. If you want to redo your vision board from time to time, go for it. It is a positive thing to update it. Your visions may change as you change. You will be amazed at how effective this exercise will be. But remember, information without implementation means absolutely nothing. It is pointless.

Information without implementation
means nothing.

Another form of vision board I have used is even more simplistic. This board uses an object as a prompt. First, begin with an idea of something you desire. Second, find a seemingly unrelated item from nature, then use it to turn that desire into a reality. This metamorphosis is truly a magical feat. Seeing something in your mind and then bringing it into your reality is amazing!

Here is how it works. Let's say that you want to have a brand-new home built from the ground up. One day you decide to go on a walk along a wood path, or on the beach, or in the mountains, or even down the street from where you live. No matter where you end up going, you find that your state of mind is completely relaxed. You are in what I call the "chill mode." Suddenly, something stands out to you—something like a stone, rock, pebble, clumps of sand, a shell on the beach, or a leaf. That something is your new focus. What others might see as just something out there in nature, you will see in your mind and use on your board and transform it into a meaningful symbol important only to you.

In your imagination, as you look at this newfound object, you see instead a finished, newly built house. In fact, it's not just a house, but a home with its rooms painted and decked out with chandeliers. You see a three-car garage with a cobblestone circle driveway that has a water fountain in the center. Do you see your house yet? Can you see your family members coming in and out of the house? Maybe you can even see the construction of this dream home and all the people working on your behalf. You begin to see it as if it truly existed. More importantly, you find a place for that stone, that leaf, that pebble, that rock or that clump of sand somewhere in your home. Literally, you take that stone and place it on your desk or on the mantel, somewhere you can see it. You take that leaf and have it shellacked onto the front door. These items have meaning only to you.

The last form of vision board is something I use every day. I call it my CPVB. This stands for the "cell phone vision board." Whether you use an Android or an iPhone, there are countless apps to help you. Photo Collage Maker and Photo Collage Editor are two very good ones. Again, the idea is first to do some soul-searching while in a very relaxed state of mind to figure out what you truly want. Like the first type of vision board, you want to create a list or collage of images and then look for ways to bring them into fruition. Look at your board as often as you can. I am not sure how many times the average person looks at his or her cell phone, but if you place your images or ideas on a lock screen, or on the home screen, then each time you use your phone, you will unlock your subconscious mind and expose it to positive images meaningful to you. Doing so will set you on a path of living out of your imagination.

Speak Life Into Yourself

As a final word, let's look at and reflect upon two of our innate abilities: listening and speaking. In my past, I listened to and heard many negative words, which I internalized. As a result, I spoke many negative words to myself and others. Sound familiar? But now you have the resources and encouragement from me to change that result by listening and speaking in a *new* way—a *positive* way, a way in which you speak life into yourself, like watering a small plant. Give yourself the best of what you need to change and grow.

My parting words are as follows: If you decide not to stop living out other people's dreams, then you need to be ready for trouble. You will continue to live in your own nightmare for as long as you choose to remain, and there will be no one responsible for that situation but you. You will, and may already be, the scariest ghost to haunt your nightmare. So, choose life. Remember that it is what you say you can do that you will do. It is what you don't say that you will not do. Begin living your new life with new thoughts!

I hope this book has helped you to...

See something different in your mirror. That difference was your image.

Look deep within yourself to find out who you are, where you are going, and why you are here.

Stop seeing yourself as other people see you no matter what negative, or even positive, opinions people have. Then stop living them and start living out your own ideas.

Find out who you are by creating a vision board and work out of the imagination gifted to you.

Simply put, living out of your own imagination is... Seeing it! Saying it! Speaking it! Believing It! Being it...while Doing it!

ABOUT THE AUTHOR
RON L. JAMES

A sought -after speaker and author, Ron James teaches, entertains and inspires audiences of all ages. His Toastmasters International speaking experience provides him with the ability to deliver humorous, yet to-the point presentations. His words make the listener become emotional about what they are hearing, and therefore, think about the circumstances surrounding their own life or the lives of people close to them.

He draws on more than 25 years of experience to teach people how to make better choices. His programs on life events, coupled with a scared-straight approach to the harsh realities of prison, will open your eyes to a place that is becoming easier and easier to get in to, but extremely difficult to get out of. Ron stirs individuals to decide on better, wiser choices for everyday life.

Today, Ron's keynote speeches, seminars, workshops and training events attract many diverse audiences from elementary school students to the 'Big Box' Retail employees and management teams, and from parents to professionals.

His book, CHOICES, was birthed as a way to inspire and help change lives.

Ron lives in Central Pennsylvania with his wife Annie and their blended families.

If this story has moved or inspired you in any way, let us know. We are here to listen to your stories and share in your life-changing moments because every choice comes with a consequence – we want you to enjoy fully the positive benefits that come with good life choices.

Ron James is eager and willing to do speaking engagements and assemblies of any size. From keynotes to Life Coaching, the content will be customized, delivered to suit your organization's specific needs.

Ron James will share his experiences with anyone – from the classroom to the boardroom – and workshops can incorporate small-group activities, role-playing, case studies, video, statistics, and in-your-face questions. Presentation materials include tailored situational stories and best-selling books.

To learn more about booking Ron James for your next meeting, training or presentation:

Visit   ronljames.com
Email   ron@ronljames.com
Call   717 433 2551
Join   Ron on Facebook: Choices with Ron James

Choices: Lessons Learned from a Repeat Offender Censored

Ronald James knows about choices, both good and bad. Unfortunately, he also knows all too well about the personal cost and tragic results that bad choices bring. After spending more than twenty-five years of his life incarcerated in a nine-by-nine cell with nothing but an uncomfortable bed, a steel toilet and sink, and a roommate, James learned one im-portant lesson: choices determine destiny.

With a determination to help others make better choices, James chronicles his emotional, heartfelt, amusing, and thought-provoking journey through his personal battles, decisions, and the consequenc-es that led him to pay the ultimate price with his life and time. As he details his experiences from an early age, James provides insight into how he developed a survival mode of thinking that evolved into a powerful tool of manipulation. He began to believe in his own lies and became deceitful in order to remove himself from tight situa-tions.

While reflecting on his own path through life and the chain of events that eventually led to his downward spiral, James encourages and empowers others to learn from his mistakes, consider their choices, and trust in God to experience a life greater than ever imagined.

Choices is a compelling, inspirational autobiography that shares life-changing wisdom for anyone who wants to begin making better choices today.

Censored
Retail: $23.95
ISBN: 978-1-945169-07-6

Uncensored—Original Version
Retail: $23.95
ISBN: 978-1-945169-06-9

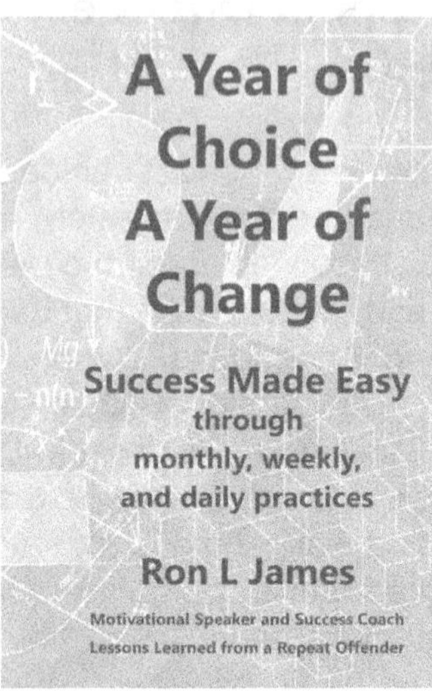

A Year of Choice A Year of Change: Success Made Easy Through Monthly, Weekly, and Daily Practices

The goal of this book is to allow you to see yourself as I see myself, which is AMAZING, so you may pursue your dreams of becoming Successful (capital S). The rules are simple: Week 1, days 1-7Allow me to speak into your imagination so that I can help you See it! (See your thoughts) Week 2, days 8-14Discover each of your dreams and follow them when you Say it! (Say the words that bring life into your being) Week 3, days 15-21Discover each of your dreams and follow them when you Speak it! (Speak life into your being) Week 4, days 22-the end of the month Become yourself when you Be It! (Walk your life out as you see it) As you reach your goals and grow into your new self, spend time with the new you. Be there for you and your family (If that means less or no time for TV, entertainment, and unfruitful vices, then so be it!) See It — Say It — Speak It — Be It This is your time. Your year. A Year of Choice, A Year of Change. Are you ready for your Success?

Retail: $19.99
ISBN: 979-8-645717-90-2

Living in Your Next Choice

Have you ever faced a situation or a prob-lem that was monumental in your life? Instead of running away or giving up. You make the choice to meet that challenge head-on and after countless hours and hard work, you find your-self victorious! That's what "Living in your Next Choice" is all about. It's the resolve of what life is all about after you've made a wise choice. Now! What will you do with your next Choice?

Retail: $10.95
ISBN: 978-1-945169-08-3

CHOICES BIBLE STUDY

This Bible Study is for you to dig deeper into the themes presented in the book and movie.
Retail: $10
ISBN: 978-1-945169-09-0

CHOICES WORKBOOK

This Workbook is designed specifically with classrooms in mind. Teachers can utilize this tool with their students in broaden the
concepts found in the movie and book as our nation faces a critical epidemic.
Retail: $10
ISBN: 978-1-945169-10-6

Business Coaching

Welcome to the world of Choices business coaching, where transformation meets success. As a business owner, you navigate through a myriad of challenges and opportunities daily. This is where a skilled business coach like me steps in, offering a roadmap to success and unlocking your full potential. Let's delve into how business coaching can revolutionize your journey:

- Accountability and Motivation: Experience heightened accountability and unwavering motivation with a coach by your side. We ensure you stay focused on your goals and hold you to your commitments, driving consistent progress.

- Increased Accountability and Focus: Harness a newfound level of accountability and razor-sharp focus. Our partnership ensures you prioritize tasks effectively, leading to improved productivity and goal achievement.

- Boosts Confidence: Embrace a confidence boost as we guide you through challenges, helping you navigate uncertainties and setbacks with resilience. Rebuild your self-assurance and tackle obstacles head-on.

- Guidance for Business Growth:** Receive expert guidance tailored to your business needs, fostering growth and expansion. From strategic planning to effective execution, we pave the way for your business's upward trajectory.

- Employee Retention Support: Foster a positive work environment and enhance employee retention with our proven strategies. Empower your team, boost morale, and create a cohesive workforce driving towards shared success.

- Strategic Business Practices: Gain insights into ideal business practices, problem-solving strategies, and goal-setting techniques. We equip you with the tools to streamline operations, optimize efficiency, and achieve sustainable growth.

- Personal and Family Support: Address personal and family issues that impact your professional life. Our holistic approach ensures a healthy work-life balance, enhancing overall well-being and productivity.

- Expert Advice and Feedback: Benefit from expert advice and constructive feedback tailored to your unique challenges. Leverage our expertise to make informed decisions and navigate complex business scenarios with confidence.

Let's embark on a transformative journey together with Ron L. James, who will empower you and your team to embrace change, unlock potential, and make every choice the best choice for your business's success. Partner with us to create a paradigm shift and realize your vision for a thriving business and a fulfilling life.

Life Coaching

I am a son, a brother, a friend, an employee, a husband, a father, a published author, a productive member of our society, a business owner, a partner, an entrepreneur, the co-founder of The Your Choice Foundation and Philanthro-pist, and now travel the world as a Keynote and Motivational Speaker ... "make your next choice your best choice."

Focus Areas:
• Addiction
• Couples Counseling
• Teenager Issues
• Anger Management

It is the hope to help individuals see themselves in a different light. Moving from where they are at to where they would like to be once a person has seen what it is they want, he helps them understand that it is their own inner voice that speaks to them to form their own belief systems that eventually they will follow. This transformation is a process that is well worth it.

Speaker

The person I am today is not the person I was back then.

I was released from prison on May 14, 2012. Since that day I have not had an alcoholic drink or chased after drugs of any sort. I have not been arrested or detained for breaking the law. As a published author I've been invited all over the United States as a motivational speaker. I have experienced the joy of legally obtaining and paying for my home and a new car. I have been involved with Toastmasters International as a featured speaker, won speech competi-tions, and been elected club president. I have a wonderful wife by my side who knows my story, accepts me for who I am today, and wants to be with me for the rest of her life! We enjoy a blended family that includes four chil-dren and three grandchildren.

How did that complete change happen? The answer is: CHOICES – good, con-scious, moral choices – and a relationship with a loving and merciful God. There are countless bad choices to be made every day, just as there are countless good choices. The choices you make today will determine your to-morrow. So make your next move your best move. Make your next choice your best choice.

CHOICES, The Movie

Please visit our website to learn more about the movie and connect with us on social media to receive updates.

www.ChoicesMovie.org

Your Choice Foundation's goal is to enrich individuals to build on their gifts to empower others.

Please send your support for this mission to:

Your Choice Foundation
1245 W Princess St.
York, PA 17404

717-433-2551

www.YourChoiceFoundation.org

www.ingramcontent.com/pod-product-compliance
Lightning Source LLC
Chambersburg PA
CBHW071440300726
48976CB00004B/1393